J
394.2
Cam
Cambell
A world of holidays

4332557
11.95

DATE DUE			

A World of Holidays!

By Louisa Campbell

Illustrated by Michael Bryant

SILVER MOON PRESS
New York

4332557

First Edition.

Designed by Cynthia Mele
Illustrated by Michael Bryant
Project Editor: Bonnie Bader

Photograph credits: p. 9 (clockwise from top): United Nations; Mary Altier; Allan Philiba; Cameramann International; p. 11: The Bettmann Archive; p. 14: Cameramann International; p. 17: Cameramann International; p. 21: Ozier Muhammad/The New York Times; p. 25: United Nations; p. 29: Mary Altier; p. 31: United Nations; p. 34: United Nations; p. 39: National Museum of the American Indian; p. 47: The Bettmann Archive; p. 50: United Nations; p. 60 (clockwise from top left): The Bettmann Archive; United Nations; United Nations; The Bettmann Archive; United Nations; Steven Fuller.

Library of Congress Cataloging-in-Publication Data

Campbell, Louisa
A World of Holidays/ By Louisa Campbell: Illustrated by Michael
  Bryant. 1st ed.
p. cm. -- (Family Ties)
ISBN 1-881889-08-4 $11.95
1. Holidays-Juvenile literature. I Bryant, Michael, ill.
II. Title. III. Series
GT3933.C36 1993
394.2'6--dc20
93-22591
CIP
AC

Many thanks to expert readers Yoshiko Nakamura of Japan, Rafat Ullah Kahn of Pakistan, Aina Iiyambo of Namibia, Louise Gibson of Canada, Audrey Shenadoah of the Onondaga nation, and Bertha Stoltzfus of Mexico.

--L.C.

A World of Holidays!

Table of Contents

Happy Days

What's your favorite day of the year? Your birthday? The Fourth of July? Christmas? All of these days celebrate something important. Christmas honors the birth of a religion. On the Fourth of July, we recall the birth of our nation. And your birthday celebrates the birth of you! Your birthday is an important day to your friends and your family, while Christmas and the Fourth of July are important to people all over the United States. Christmas is also celebrated in many places outside the United States. Christmas and the Fourth of July are examples of public holidays. On these days, schools and offices are often closed. People celebrate with ceremonies, parades and parties.

This book is about holidays in other countries. (Some of these occasions are also observed in the United States. Which ones do you recognize?) The stories show how children take part in holiday celebrations with their families and their communities.

On holidays we take a break from our normal routines. These days give us time to focus on our families, our communities, our nations, or our religions. But most of all, we can have fun on holidays! So now, let's take a look at how people in other places honor these special times.

Holidays are all around us — all the time!

New Year's Holidays

People all over the world celebrate the new year. The New Year's holiday in the United States is celebrated on January 1. On that day, Americans gather with their families to watch football games and parades. They also follow the custom of making New Year's resolutions — giving up bad habits and making new beginnings while the year is still fresh.

Not all countries use the same calendar that those of us in the West do. The Chinese, for example, have their own way of counting days and months. The Chinese base their calendar on the Moon, while ours is based on the Sun. That's why their New Year comes at a different time from the Western New Year. Chinese New Year comes in winter, and the celebration lasts for fifteen days.

Chinese New Year is often celebrated with a lively, noisy parade, and lots of firecrackers. Dancers dressed up as a big dragon lead the parade. The dragon dance is thought to bring luck in the new year.

Like the Chinese, many people look for

signs of luck at the beginning of the year. On January 1 the Scottish greet the "first footer" — the first person to enter the house in the new year. His or her looks are said to foreshadow the year's fortune. If the "first footer" is tall, with dark hair and dark eyes, the Scots predict that the new year will be a happy one.

There are many other ways of celebrating the new year. In Ecuador, families make "Año Viejo" ("Old Year") dummies for New Year's Eve. The dummies are stuffed with straw, like scarecrows. At midnight the "Año Viejo" is set on fire. The burning of the "Año Viejo" is a very dramatic way to say goodbye to any problems and sadness of the year that has passed.

The following story is about a girl in Japan and a New Year's Eve celebration. She will learn how to say goodbye to the problems of the old year and welcome the new year.

Lanterns are an exciting part of the Chinese New Year Parade. So are elaborate costumes and streets crowded with people.

The Beautiful Birds

Twelve-year-old Midori stood on a stepladder outside her house. Carefully, she tacked a bunch of pine, palm and bamboo over the front door. The green, leafy decoration was created specially for *Shogatsu,* the Japanese New Year. Midori stood on her toes and put her nose next to the sprigs. They smelled like the forest. Her grandmother had explained that the greenery brought good luck for Shogatsu.

Stepping down, Midori stood back to admire the decorated doorway. "Perfect!" she thought.

It was five o'clock on New Year's Eve. Midori's family, like everyone else in Japan, had been working hard to get ready for the Shogatsu holidays. By tonight all school and office work must be finished. Every house must be clean and tidy, inside and out.

Midori was very excited about the holidays.

Tonight she and her two little brothers would stay up past their usual bedtimes. In fact, the whole family would be awake long after midnight to welcome in the first hours of the new year.

After dinner, she would put on her kimono and go to the shrine with her family. Shogatsu was the one time of year when everyone dressed in kimonos. Most of Midori's friends had bought theirs at stores, but her grandmother had sewn Midori's. She had even let Midori pick out the material herself — cream-colored silk printed with blue and gold and orange birds. The kimono was tied with a bright blue sash.

Over the last few weeks, Midori had watched while Grandmother had sewn the kimono. Grandmother showed Midori how to measure and cut the silk, and then how to pin and stitch all the pieces together. Grandmother had left one sleeve for Midori to finish all by herself.

Midori brought the kimono to her room to complete the sleeve. She took her sewing basket from her night table. It was difficult to thread the needle because the silk thread was so fine, but Midori had had lots of practice. She sewed quickly, making small, invisible stitches, just as Grandmother had taught her.

"Midori!" her mother called. "It's time for supper. Hurry, or we will be late getting to the shrine."

"Yes, Mother," Midori said. "I'm coming." Luckily, she had just finished hemming the sleeve. She tied a tiny knot and snipped the thread. Then she folded her kimono carefully, put it on her bed, and left the room.

The rest of the family was already at the table. Midori's father sat at one end of the table. Her mother brought in the dishes and set them down. Grandmother helped pass them around. Midori's little brothers, Hideto, who

A Japanese girl in a traditional kimono.

was five, and Hitoshi, aged six, immediately began to eat the New Year's Eve meal. There were bowls of soup, extra-long, thin noodles, and tea. But Midori was so excited she couldn't eat a thing. With her chopsticks she poked at the noodles and pushed them around her bowl. Her mind was on her kimono.

"Eat your noodles, Midori," Grandmother said with a smile. "They will stretch your good luck far into the new year." But all Midori could think of was the beautiful kimono with the blue and gold and orange birds.

After supper, Midori rushed back to her room to change. Carefully, she put on her kimono and wrapped it closed with the sash. She ran into her parents' room and stood in front of the full-length mirror. Midori felt like the birds. She was ready to take off!

Then something caught Midori's eye. "No," she gasped. "It can't be true!" She lifted her arms and compared her two sleeves in the mirror. Yes, it was true. The sleeve that Midori had sewn was too long. And, it was crooked! "I've ruined my kimono!" she thought.

"Midori!" her father called. "Come! Everyone is ready." Midori rushed out of the house to the car for the short ride to the shrine. She was very anxious.

They arrived and parked the car. Waves of people moved up the many steps to the shrine, a large wooden building with a sloped roof. Midori didn't want to join them, even though all her friends were in the crowd. She was afraid Grandmother would be disappointed with her for having done such a poor job of sewing.

But Midori knew she had to join the celebration. No one had noticed the uneven sleeves yet. Maybe, if she was careful, they wouldn't. Midori stood behind her mother and grandmother. Their kimonos were perfect, of course!

Hideto and Hitoshi were already taking part in the Shogatsu celebration. They ran to get their fortunes, which were given away outside the shrine every year at Shogatsu. The fortunes were printed on white paper ribbons. Hideto looked at his fortune: *The new year will bring you wealth.* Hideto smiled. "I'm going to be rich!" he shouted. Hitoshi's fortune read, *In the new year you will be healthy and strong.* "And I'm going to be a muscle man!" shrieked Hitoshi. Mother, Father, and Grandmother laughed.

The boys ran to tie their fortunes to a small tree. There were already many other fortunes tied to the bare branches. The pretty white ribbons made the tree look as if it were full of blossoms. Midori smiled. The fortune tree reminded Midori of bright spring, even though it was dark winter.

On the way to the shrine on Shogatsu.

Next the family climbed the stairs to visit the long-life flame — a torch at the shrine that never went out. Father had brought a rope to catch a spark. They would carry the smoldering rope home and use it to light their stove. Then they would cook the first meal of the new year. "A spark from the long-life flame will keep sickness away." Grandmother said. She knew all the customs.

It was now almost midnight. As Midori and her family waited their turn for a spark, Midori

17

felt happy. She had practically forgotten about her kimono. And fortunately, no one had noticed her crooked sleeve! Midori realized she had been selfish to think that her problem was so important. No one was paying attention to just Midori.

Midori looked around at all the other women and at the hundreds of gorgeous kimonos. She looked down at hers. The blue and gold and orange birds were truly lovely. Midori knew that she could take out the hem on her sleeve and resew it. And her grandmother would help her. Her kimono would be perfect for next year. But for this year, it would be all right.

Midori looked over at her grandmother. As usual, Grandmother was chuckling over some joke. Midori laughed, too. Then Midori looked at her handsome parents and her lively little brothers. She was proud of her family, and she was proud of herself.

The crowd grew silent. It was midnight. The shrine's huge gong was struck by the monks who lived and worked at the shrine. *Chong! Chong! Chong!* Many times the gong tolled. Midori remembered what Grandmother had told her about the New Year's Eve gong. The

tolling meant that the mistakes of the past were
forgiven. Listening to the gong, Midori felt like
the beautiful blue and gold and orange birds —
happy and bright and ready to soar into the new
year.

Ramadan and Eid-ul-Fitr

Islam is a religion, and those who follow it are known as Muslims. There are Muslims all over the world; many of them live in countries in Africa, Asia, and the Middle East. As in other religions, there are many holidays and celebrations in Islam. But the most important time of year for Muslims is Ramadan, the name of the ninth month of the Islamic calendar.

During Ramadan most adults, teenagers, and even some children fast during the daylight hours. Fasting is an important part of many religions. Have you ever given up anything you love, like TV or chocolate, if only for a short time? Many religions believe that doing without something you take for granted makes you appreciate the things you have.

At the end of Ramadan, Muslims are proud and happy to have completed their fasting. To celebrate, they have a three-day holiday, called Eid-ul-Fitr.

In many Muslim countries Eid-ul-Fitr is a special time for children. In Turkey, a country in the Middle East, Eid-ul-Fitr is known as "the candy holiday." Children receive candy and coins wrapped in colorful handkerchiefs.

In the North African country of Sudan, grownups give children candy dolls that hold beautiful paper fans on Eid-ul-Fitr. Many families save and collect these fans to remind them of the holidays.

Eid-ul-Fitr begins with a new moon at the start of the month. The new moon can also be found on the flag of many countries where most of the people are Muslims.

The following story is about the new moon and a family in Pakistan.

Chapter Three

Pakistani families often gather to celebrate Eid-ul-Fitr together. Everyone gets to take part.

The New Moon

Mahmood! Look, Mahmood!" little Khalid squealed, pointing up at the sky. "There it is! I see it! There's the new moon!" The boys were standing with their parents on the roof of their apartment building.

Mahmood ignored his younger brother, and continued scanning the sky. Khalid couldn't possibly have seen the moon. He wasn't even looking in the right direction.

As the sky grew darker, Mahmood was able to make out a pale sliver of a moon. "The new moon has risen in the sky!" Mahmood shouted. "Everyone, look! Mother, Father, Khalid, there it is! There's the moon!"

Happy shouts and cries rose up from the street and the other roofs. People hugged each other. Firecrackers crackled and sparkled. The holy month of Ramadan was over. No more fasting. The three-day celebration of Eid-ul-Fitr would begin tomorrow. It was time for Muslims in Pakistan and all over the world to give thanks and to celebrate.

And now there was so much to do! "Come, children!" said Mahmood's mother. "Let's go to the bazaar right away."

Mahmood knew that it was time to buy special holiday foods and new clothing for Eid. Tomorrow everyone must be dressed in brand new clothes from head to foot.

After a short walk, the excited family arrived at the lively, noisy bazaar. There were rows of stalls piled high with food, clothing, jewelry, pots and pans — all kinds of wonderful things to buy. Behind the stalls, merchants, both men and women, shouted to people to come buy what they had to sell. Customers pushed and shoved to get to their favorite stalls.

"I've left everything for the last minute this year!" Mother said with a smile. "Mahmood, you'll have to watch Khalid. Your father and I must concentrate on this shopping list. Tarooq, what do you think of these vests for the boys?"

Just then, Mahmood noticed his favorite treat at a nearby stall. His stomach growled. He dashed over to the stall. What luck! He had just enough money to buy one of the treats. The sticky, yummy pastry tasted even more delicious than usual. "Probably because I've been fasting," thought Mahmood.

This was the first year Mahmood was old enough to join in the Ramadan fast. For four days, during the daylight hours, Mahmood had not had a thing to eat or drink — not even a sip of water. The adults fasted each day, from dawn to dusk, for the entire month! Fasting had made Mahmood feel very grown up.

Suddenly, Mahmood remembered Khalid. Where was he? Mahmood spun around. He looked in all directions. He had forgotten his little brother! Where had Khalid gone? Mahmood panicked. He ran back to his parents. They had just bought the boys fancy new vests for Eid. Khalid was not there. He was lost! Mahmood certainly did not feel very grown up now.

Mother was upset. Father was angry. But there was no time to scold Mahmood. They must find little Khalid. Each went off in a different direction.

Mahmood ran down the center aisle of the bazaar. He asked the young man selling copper pots. No Khalid. He asked the old man selling gold and silver jewelry. No Khalid. Mahmood darted in and out of the stalls. He did not even see the colorful displays of fruits and spices. He did not even notice the candies and cassette tapes and clothes piled on the stalls. All Mahmood knew was that Khalid was nowhere to be found!

A crowded market in Pakistan.

Suddenly, Mahmood felt a strong hand on his shoulder. He jumped! It was Father. "I'm taking you home and you will stay there. There's no point in losing both you boys," he said sternly.

Father guided Mahmood through the crowds. All the way home, Mahmood worried about his little brother. "If I were old enough to fast this year, then I should be old enough to take care of my little brother," Mahmood thought.

But when they arrived at their house, Mahmood could not believe his eyes. Khalid was sitting on the stoop, humming to himself! Father scooped the little boy up in his arms and gave him a big hug. "Silly, silly Khalid!" he said with relief. "We thought we'd lost you!"

"I'm so sorry, Father!" Mahmood blurted out. "I forgot to watch Khalid."

"Never mind for now, Mahmood," Father answered. "It's Eid, and it's a time for happiness. You boys go inside. I'll go back to the bazaar and tell your mother that everything's all right. After all, we still have lots of shopping to do."

Then he gave Mahmood a smile and a wink. "Do take care of your little brother this time!"

And that's just what Mahmood did. The next morning, Mahmood got up early and helped Khalid put on his brand new clothes — an embroidered vest and loose, light cotton pants and shirt. At breakfast there was only enough for one boy to have a second helping of the special Eid noodle dish called Sawaeen. It was tasty and sweet with dates, raisins, almonds, and pistachios. Mahmood wanted to eat it all himself, but he shared it with his little brother.

When it was time to go to the mosque to pray, Mahmood asked Father if Khalid could go along. Khalid did not usually go to the mosque with Mahmood and Father because he was too young. But Father said it would be all right, since today was a special occasion. Mahmood and Khalid smiled.

The boys walked proudly alongside their father. Outside the mosque each family gave money to the beggars. Father and Mahmood handed Khalid some coins. Then Khalid gave the money away to a poor man. This duty made little Khalid feel very important!

Father, Mahmood, and Khalid joined the

other men in washing their faces, hands, and feet before entering the mosque. Their shoes were left outside. Then they took their places behind the prayer leader. At certain times, everyone had to kneel and pray and chant after the leader.

When they returned home, aunts and uncles and cousins and friends visited throughout the afternoon. All the grownups gave Mahmood, Khalid, and the other children Eidi — holiday gifts of money.

That night, Khalid and Mahmood were allowed to take their shiny, new coins, called "Eidi coins," and go to the Eid carnival. Mahmood let Khalid decide which ride they would go on first. Khalid picked the Ferris wheel. After standing in line, the brothers stepped onto the ride and were strapped into the swinging car. The gears creaked and the Ferris wheel started to spin. Up, up, up! Mahmood and Khalid flew through the sky. As their car reached the very top, the Ferris wheel stopped.

"Mahmood, look! There it is again. I see it! The new moon!" said Khalid. "See! It's a little fatter now." Just then the first colorful fireworks display exploded in the evening sky.

The brothers watched the entire Eid fireworks show from the top of the Ferris wheel, high above the carnival crowd. As the bright colors lit the sky, Mahmood glanced at his little brother. Khalid was smiling widely, entranced by the show. Mahmood thought he and Khalid had the best seats anywhere for watching the Eid fireworks display!

Mahmood grinned. "What could be better?" he thought. "I have a loving family and a wonderful life!" Mahmood counted his blessings. That was what Eid was about, after all. Mahmood took his little brother's hand and gave it a happy squeeze.

A group of Arab musicians, around the time of the holiday celebration.

National Holidays

In the United States, the Fourth of July is a time to celebrate our nation's freedom. Before our country rebelled and became an independent nation, it was a group of colonies governed by England. Colonies are often controlled by a government in a far-away place. A nation is a group of people in one place that controls its own government.

Many other nations were once colonies, and today they celebrate their freedom, too. For example, India, which was once controlled by Britain, celebrates its independence on August 15. And Mexico, which was once governed by Spain, celebrates its independence on September 16. In France, the national holiday is July 14, Bastille Day, when the people celebrate their liberty and their national unity.

Namibia, a country in southwestern Africa, was once a colony controlled first by Germany and then later by South Africa.

The Germans and the South Africans treated the Namibian people badly. South Africa ruled through its own system of laws, which included *apartheid.* Apartheid segregated people according to the color of their skin and discriminated against black Namibians. The people of Namibia rebelled against South Africa's colonial rule. After fighting a long war, the Namibians got their independence. Now Namibia is a nation, and the people celebrate their independence on March 21.

Although Namibia is a nation, most of the people in the country, as in many African nations, belong to tribes. Tribes are made up of people who are related by family ties and traditions. Tribes existed in Namibia long before it was a nation and long before it was a colony, and the tribes remain important in modern Namibia.

The following story is about a boy, his family, and the celebration of his nation's independence.

Every kid in the neighborhood can get involved in national celebrations.

The Great Day

Click. Paandu's mother turned off the light and glanced over at the bed. Nine-year-old Paandu lay quietly, pretending to be asleep. When his mother had left the room and had closed the door, he slipped out of bed and found his flashlight. He shined it on his new jeans to admire them once again. Then he unfolded his new shirt and held it up. Paandu was thrilled. Now he had a Michael Jackson tee shirt of his very own!

Cousin Jerry had bought the tee shirt at a real Michael Jackson concert in New York. Jerry had sent the tee shirt and jeans all the way to Namibia for Paandu's birthday last week. Carefully he placed the shirt back in the box. The box was covered with American postage stamps. Paandu planned to keep the box forever.

Paandu switched off the flashlight and slipped back into bed. But he was too excited to sleep. Tomorrow was Independence Day, and he would get to wear his new American clothes for the first time! Paandu thought about how he would look marching with the Boys' Club in the Independence Day parade. Everyone would be looking at his new clothes! Later, he and his family would have braai, a delicious barbecue — chicken, beef, and lamb — with all their friends. "It will be a great day!" thought Paandu happily.

Paandu lay in bed thinking about the talk his father had given that day at school. He told the class how he and Paandu's mum had fought in the war for independence. Paandu knew how long and hard the people of Namibia had struggled. There had been apartheid when South Africa had ruled. And before that, the Germans had colonized Namibia. His father had told him many times how terrible life was when Namibia was not free! Paandu had heard that speech many, many times. Finally, Paandu settled into bed and drifted off to sleep.

The next morning his mother shook him awake. "Paandu! Paandu! You slept through breakfast. Wake up! The parade starts soon. Hurry now! We'll be waiting outside."

Paandu sat up and stretched his arms. How

Celebrations of nationhood are times of parades and pageantry.

could he have over-slept? Probably because he had stayed up so late thinking. He jumped out of bed and ran into the bathroom to wash his face. Then he zipped up his new jeans and pulled his new Michael Jackson tee shirt on over his head. With a big grin he dashed to the kitchen, grabbed a piece of toast, and ran outside.

His father looked at Paandu. "What have you got on, son?" he hollered. "Put on your costume this instant!"

Mum hurried Paandu back to his room. She was cross. "Paandu! You know perfectly well you should be wearing your Owambus costume for the parade!" Owambus was the name of their tribe.

"But Mum," Paandu protested, "I wanted everyone to see my new American clothes."

"Don't be silly! You can't wear American clothes to perform Owambus dances! You can change your clothes later for braai if you want to."

Paandu sighed and slowly took off his new jeans. Then, he put on his costume. It was a traditional garment that draped across his shoulder. Around his neck he wore a string of black beads. Underneath the costume, he kept his Michael Jackson tee shirt on. He ran back out the door carrying his jeans.

Paandu joined his friends at the start of the parade. All the other boys were bare chested. "Come on now," said Mum. "Take off that tee shirt and give it to me. I'll take care of it."

Paandu scowled as he pulled off his tee shirt and handed it to his mother. "Some great day," he grumbled.

The drums began to beat, softly at first then louder. Paandu and his club took their place in the parade. All twenty-three boys started to dance. They had been practicing for weeks. Stomp-stomp-stomp-twirl. Stomp-stomp-stomp-twirl.

Paandu could feel the beads around his neck bounce to the beat. He could feel the leather fringe around his waist shake. He could feel the earth through the soles of his bare feet as they pounded against the dirt road. Stomp-stomp-stomp-twirl. Stomp-stomp-stomp-twirl. Faster and faster. Paandu's friends smiled and laughed as they danced. Paandu began to smile, too.

The crowd lining the road clapped and shouted. They cheered on the Boys' Club. Everybody at the Independence Day parade loved the dancing. Paandu was no longer in a bad mood. In fact, now he was in a really good mood. The boys and their Owambus dances were a big hit!

When the parade ended, the Boys' Club posed for a photograph. Tired and happy, the boys stood arm-in-arm in their Owambus costumes. Paandu looked down at his beads and his clothes. He thought about how his grandfather had dressed like this every day of his life, and his great-grandfather before him. On and on, back to the beginning of history, Owambus warriors had worn clothes like this. The Owambus and other tribes had always lived here in Namibia. Paandu felt proud to be a Namibian.

The picture-taking session ended. Paandu's mother and father came up to him. Dad picked Paandu up off the ground in a big bear hug. "Wonderful dancing, son! The nation is proud of you and the Boys' Club."

"Here you are, Paandu," said Mum. She handed Paandu his American clothes.

"Will you hold onto them, please?" asked Paandu. "I want to wear my costume!"

"Oh, ho-ho!" chuckled Dad. Then he laughed. Paandu laughed, too. Then he rushed ahead to join his friends as they ran to the Independence Day braai.

Harvest Festivals

People all over the world give thanks at harvest times. Harvests produce food, and without food people could not survive. In India the harvest takes place during the month of October, when the farmers bring in their crops. At that time, they lay down their plows and decorate them with garlands of flowers to celebrate the harvest.

During the harvest season, people celebrate the Thanksgiving holiday. They give thanks for many things. For instance, in the United States Virgin Islands there is a Hurricane Thanksgiving. On that day people give thanks for having lived through the hurricane season.

On Thanksgiving day in the United States and Canada, people give thanks for all the good things of the past year. It is also a time to remember the first European settlers who came to America and their struggles to survive.

Native-Americans often helped the early settlers with their planting, since Native-Americans knew how to farm the soil. In many cases the settlers' harvests would have failed without the help of the Native-Americans. If the harvests had failed, the settlers would not have been able to survive in the new land.

The following story is about Thanksgiving in Canada, and a young girl and her Native-American godmother.

As in many other celebration in other cultures, food is a vital part of many Native-American holiday gatherings.

The Three Sifters

The day after tomorrow would be the Canadian Thanksgiving. Ten-year-old Winona loved helping her parents prepare for the holiday. Her favorite job was making a centerpiece for the table. First, Winona would arrange spikes of barley, wheat, and oats in her mother's best silver vase. Then she would surround the vase with apples and pears and grapes so that the colors looked just right. The grains and fruits symbolized the fall harvest. Each year Winona tried to make her arrangement more beautiful than the year before.

Winona also loved helping her parents prepare the special meal. Her mother would roast a plump turkey and her father would make other holiday dishes, like Winona's favorite, sweet potatoes topped with tiny marshmallows. But this year her father had broken his arm, so he would not be able to do any cooking. That's why Auntie was coming up to Canada from

New York to help with the meal.

Auntie was Winona's godmother. She often came for holidays, but not usually for Thanksgiving. Winona didn't quite know why. It had something to do with her being an American Indian. Winona knew that Auntie was an Iroquois. She had learned about the Iroquois in school, but whenever she said Iroquois, Auntie corrected her. "Haudenosaunee is the name of our people. Iroquois is what outsiders call us," Auntie said.

When Auntie arrived, she carried a huge bag of vegetables from her own garden. "What is that for, Auntie?" Winona asked.

"For cooking, of course," answered Auntie. "You'll see tomorrow. It's about time you met the three sisters, little one."

Winona did not listen to everything Auntie said. She was too busy thinking that her family would not be having their usual Thanksgiving meal. She saw that Auntie was not planning to cook the same dishes her father always cooked. The vegetables Auntie had brought were boring. "Corn, beans, and squash," thought Winona. "Ugh."

The next day at school Winona remembered what Auntie had said. "It's about time you met the three sisters." What was Auntie talking about? Auntie had never mentioned any sisters before. Had she invited her three sisters for Thanksgiving?

When Winona arrived home from school, her parents were still away at work. But Auntie was busy cooking in the kitchen. Auntie looked up from the stove, and smiled. Then she tied an apron around Winona's waist. "Rats," Winona thought. "Auntie's going to make me eat her weird food and cook it, too." But Winona knew that complaining would get her nowhere.

Soon Winona was too busy even to think about complaining. She and Auntie chopped and stirred and mashed and rolled. They added milk and nuts and berries to the mixtures. Then they boiled and baked them. They worked all afternoon. They made cornbread and dumplings and tamales and cakes and pudding. Surprisingly, Winona realized she was enjoying herself. "Auntie, this is fun," she said.

"Sure it's fun," said Auntie. "The three sisters are a gift from the creator."

"Auntie!" cried Winona. "WHO ARE THE THREE SISTERS?"

"Corn, beans, and squash, of course," answered Auntie. She looked at Winona and laughed. "I bet you didn't know that vegetables had sisters! Come, let's rest for a moment." Winona sat on Auntie's floury lap.

"Let me tell you about the harvest," Auntie began. "The harvest comes from the Earth, our home. We live here, but we do not own the Earth. It belongs to the creator. The Earth offers us medicine from plants, food like the three sisters, and delicious treats like strawberries and maple syrup. Each time I harvest from the creator's garden, I give thanks. Haudenosaunee Thanksgiving comes many times during the

43

year."

"Is that why you never come to our Canadian Thanksgiving?" asked Winona.

"Yes," answered Auntie, "that is one of the reasons. The other reason is that your Thanksgiving celebrates the coming of the English and the Europeans to this continent. That is not an event that we Haudenosaunee are particularly happy about."

"But Daddy is English," said Winona. "Don't you like him?"

"Of course I do, Winona. Your father and I have been friends for a long time. But still, Canadian Thanksgiving is not my holiday."

Winona's face fell. She was thinking that Auntie would be unhappy tomorrow. Auntie noticed that Winona seemed sad.

"Don't worry, little one. I will celebrate with you tomorrow. It won't be Thanksgiving to me, but it will be a lovely party with my dear friends — you and your parents!"

Winona nodded. "From now on, tomorrow's not Thanksgiving, it's Three Sisters' Day!"

"No, no, Winona! Tomorrow can be one thing to me and another to you."

"So, then why can't it be both things to

me?" insisted Winona. "Why can't tomorrow be both Thanksgiving and Three Sisters' Day?"

"That sounds fine to me. You've got a deal!" said Auntie. "Now back to work!"

The next morning Winona woke up early. Her mother roasted the turkey. Auntie put the finishing touches on her Haudenosaunee dishes. And Winona worked on her centerpiece for the table. She was just as careful as always. But this time she added vegetables from Auntie's garden — ears of corn, bunches of green beans, and funny-shaped squashes.

When her father saw the table he said, "How wonderful, Winona! This is your most beautiful centerpiece ever!"

"Thanks," said Winona, smiling at Auntie. "Have you met the three sisters?"

Christmas

Christmas is one of the most important times of the year in the Christian religion. On this day, Christians celebrate in church the birth of Jesus Christ with songs, prayers, and pageants. There are many holiday traditions in homes as well, like the arrival of Santa Claus, decorating the Christmas tree, enjoying a special dinner, singing carols and exchanging presents.

In Europe and North America, Christmas comes during winter, which is the darkest time of the year in those regions. There is not much light. Many Christmas traditions honor the gift of light. These traditions remind people that the long, warmer days of the spring will come again.

In Sweden the Christmas celebration begins on December 13 when young girls wear crowns bright with tiny lights. Do you know of any holiday traditions that celebrate light? In some countries, candles are placed in windows during Christmas. These lights honor the story of Joseph and Mary and their journey to

Chapter Six

Bethlehem to give birth to Jesus.

Children in Germany celebrate "Knocking Nights," when they wear costumes and go to other houses in their neighborhoods for candy.

In France, it is traditional to have a supper, called the *reveillon,* right after midnight on Christmas Eve.

In Mexico, a Christmas tradition called Las Posadas also remembers the journey of Mary and Joseph. Las Posadas refers to the place where Jesus was born. Las Posadas is also the name for the special celebrations that take place during the nine days before Christmas in Mexico.

The following story is about a Mexican girl and her family during Las Posadas.

Sleds, warm clothes, wrapped presents, and kids — all the things that make Christmas fun for many people in the world.

The Marvelous Time

Eleven-year-old Rosa was unhappy as she listened to her mother talking on the phone to Aunt Dolores, who lived in New York. "Si, si! Las Posadas has been wonderful this year! It's just like when we were children. The girls are having a marvelous time!"

Mama continued to chat and Rosa continued to sulk. The girl, thought Rosa, not girls. Yes, maybe Lourdes, Rosa's older sister, was having a marvelous time. But not Rosa.

In Mexico, Las Posadas was celebrated during the nine days before Christmas. During this time, there were parties, called *fiestas,* every night. And this year, the grown-ups had decided to bring back the old custom of having a parade on each of the nine nights of Las Posadas.

Rosa's mother finally hung up the phone. "Put your costume on, Rosa! It is almost time for tonight's parade."

With a long face, Rosa went slowly to her room to change into her angel costume. She thought about the last few weeks. She had to admit that the days leading up to Las Posadas had been marvelous. Mama had taken Rosa and her sister to visit an artist, who was making big, papier-mache figures of the nativity — Maria, Jose, and baby Jesus. The artist even made animals for the stable — an ox, pigs, cows and chickens. A young girl and boy would be chosen to carry the figures of Maria and Jose in the Posadas parades.

The grown-ups selected the girl to carry the figure of Maria. It was Lourdes, who was twelve! Rosa's older sister would lead each parade. Yes, thought Rosa, Posadas had been marvelous until that moment. That's when Rosa realized that Lourdes was to be the center of attention for all of Las Posadas! It wasn't fair.

Tonight was the eighth night of the holiday. To Rosa the eight nights had seemed like eight years. She took her usual place as an angel at the back of the parade. Of course, all the other angels were much younger than Rosa.

Each angel held a candle. With a long match, Mama lit each one. "Give us a smile, Rosa. Don't look so glum." Rosa gave her mother a big phony smile, but Mama wasn't fooled. She

Christmas religious celebrations are times to dress up, but also times to laugh with friends.

just shook her head and smiled. "Rosa, Rosa! What am I to do with you?"

Mama joined Papa and the other grown-ups in the parade. They all carried colored lanterns. Pink, green, and yellow light danced around as the people marched through the dark streets of the town. Rosa tried not to look at Lourdes, but there she was, at the very front of the procession. Proudly, Lourdes carried the big, beautiful figure of Maria high above her head.

The parade stopped at the large, white house of Señor and Señora Garcia. Lourdes knocked on the door. The Garcias pretended to be surprised when the whole parade burst into song. "Is there room at the inn?" the crowd sang. "Is there a place for a pregnant woman to rest? She and her husband have travelled far!"

Señor and Señora Garcia sang the next verse of the Posadas song. "No, the inn is full. There is no room at the inn!"

Next the angels sang alone. "Can't you see? It is Santa Maria, Queen of Heaven, who stands at your door! Please! Let her in!"

Finally, the Garcias sang the last verse. "Very well, come in. Perhaps we can find a place in the stable. But the couple will have to sleep in the hay with the animals!"

The Garcias opened their doors wide. The whole parade marched in through the house to the courtyard. There was the manger, with all the papier-mache animals gathered around. Everyone watched as Lourdes laid the figure of Santa Maria down. And then, like every night of Las Posadas, the fiesta began.

Rosa took a cup of fruit punch and went to sit by herself in a corner. She hoped no one would notice her. She burned with jealousy. Why did Lourdes have to be the one to carry Santa Maria every single night?

Just then, Lourdes ran up to her younger sister. "Rosa, I've been looking everywhere for you. Señora Garcia says you can have first crack at the pinata!"

Rosa did not even care, but she went along anyway. Señora Garcia gave Rosa a bat, blind-folded her, and then spun her around three times. Rosa swung weakly. She completely missed the brightly painted, frilly, crepe paper donkey that hung overhead in the center of the room. Everyone laughed. Of course, when it was her turn, Lourdes hit the piñata dead-center and smashed it open! Rosa didn't even go to take her share of the pieces of candy and little toys that came spilling out of the broken piñata.

The next day Rosa avoided Lourdes. Rosa was so jealous she could hardly stand the sight of her older sister. At least it would all be over tomorrow, thought Rosa. Maybe next year Rosa would be the one chosen to carry the Santa Maria.

Just as Rosa was thinking these thoughts, Lourdes came up to her carrying a strange looking bundle, wrapped up in paper and string. "Here, Rosa, this is for you."

"Maybe it's Santa Maria!" thought Rosa. "Maybe tonight I will take Lourdes's part!"

Quickly Rosa unwrapped the package. It wasn't the beautiful figure of Santa Maria. It was the beautiful figure of baby Jesus!

"Tonight is Christmas Eve, the last night of Las Posadas," explained Lourdes. "On Christmas Eve, baby Jesus joins us. And everyone wants you, Rosa, to carry him, because you are the oldest angel. Tonight, you and the baby Jesus will lead the Posadas parade!"

Rosa felt very happy. She also felt very embarrassed. But she knew what to do. She apologized. "I'm sorry that I've been so jealous, Lourdes. I don't know what got into me!"

Lourdes answered, "It's okay, little sister. Everybody feels jealous once in a while. Tonight you'll see that, during Las Posadas, all children play important parts. Even little sisters!"

Rosa corrected Lourdes. "Even jealous little sisters!" Now both sisters were ready to enjoy the marvelous holiday time.

Año Viejo

A New Year's Eve custom in Ecuador. Families make Año Viejo dummies and set them on fire at midnight.

apartheid

A system of laws used by the South African government to separate white people from black people. The laws discriminate against black people.

braai

An outdoor, southern African barbecue party; or the name for a barbecued food. Chicken, lamb, and beef are the most popular barbecued meats.

colony

A country of people that is controlled by a government that is not its own.

discriminate against

To treat people unfairly.

Eid-ul-Fitr

The holiday that takes place when Ramadan ends. Also known as Eid.

Eidi

Presents of money given to children on Eid-ul-Fitr.

fast

To go without food or water for a certain amount of time.

fiesta
The Spanish word for a party.

first footer
The first person to enter the house in the new year in Scotland.

Haudenosaunee
A group of six Native-American Indian tribes also known as the Iroquois.

Iroquois
See Haudenosaunee.

Islam
The religion that Muslims follow. They believe that there is one God, Allah, and Mohammed is his prophet.

kimono
A long robe with wide sleeves and sash. It is the national costume of Japan.

Las Posadas
The holidays that take place during the eight nights and nine days before Christmas in Mexico.

manger
A box from which horses or cows eat. The Bible says that Jesus was born in a stable and given a manger filled with straw for a bed.

mosque
A place of worship for Muslims.

Glossary

Muslim
A person who follows the religion of Islam.

nation
A group of people in one place that controls its own government.

Owambus
The largest tribe in Namibia.

papier-mache
Lightweight molding material of paper and glue for making sculptures.

piñata
A colorful, frilly paper figure filled with candy and toys.

Ramadan
The ninth and most important month of the Islamic calendar. Muslims fast during this time.

reveillon
A traditional supper in France, served right after midnight mass on Christmas Eve.

Shogatsu
The holidays that take place in Japan at the start of the new year.

resolution
A promise to give up bad habits and make new beginnings.

Sawaeen
An Eid noodle dish made from dates, raisins, almonds, and pistachios.

shrine
A place of worship in Japan.

tribe
A group of people related by family ties and traditions.

CREATE A WORLD OF HOLIDAYS CALENDAR

Have you ever taken part in a holiday celebration? Then you know how much fun they can be. You also know that there are lots of holidays during the year. And that they can be hard to keep track of! A good way to remember all the holidays and special days throughout the year is to make your own calendar. Here's how:

✱ The first thing you'll need is a calendar. You can either buy one in a store, or make one yourself. Borrow a calendar from a friend, or family member, or even the library, and copy each month on a separate piece of paper. You can use pretty markers, crayons, or paints. Then, staple or glue the pages together.

✱ The first date you'll want to fill in is your birthday! You can draw a picture of a birthday cake and write your name or your age on that date. Then, in the proper places, fill in the birthdays of all your friends and relatives. It could also be fun to fill in anniversaries or other special family celebrations, like reunions.

✳ Next, fill in the dates of national holidays. For the Fourth of July, for example, you can draw fireworks and an American flag. For Thanksgiving, which is celebrated on the fourth Thursday of November, you can draw a turkey. What other national holidays can you think of?

✳ Now it's time to add the religious holidays. If you celebrate Christmas, it always falls on December 25. But if you celebrate Hanukkah, it falls on a different day each year. Try to find out when it is celebrated in the year you're working on. Of course, there are lots of other religious holidays to note: Easter, Passover, Ramadan.

Activity

✳ It is also fun to find other holidays throughout the year. Valentine's Day falls on February 14. Memorial Day is observed on the last Monday in May. And Halloween is celebrated on October 31.

✳   After you've finished filling in all the holidays you celebrate, go back and find some of the holidays you've learned about in this book. Canadian Thanksgiving falls on the second Monday in October. Namibia Independence Day is on August 15. What other holidays do you want to include in your calendar?

✳   Many holidays don't fall on the same day each year. Two good books to look in to find out when the holidays fall in a specific year are *The World Almanac,* or *Chase's Annual Events.* Your librarian will be able to give you a copy of these books.

✳ Finally, your *World of Holidays* calendar makes a great present! You can give it to family and friends to celebrate a special time.

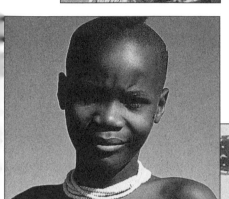

all live a world of different faces,
ilies, and holiday celebrations.
ere does your face fit into this page?